SLAVE SONG

Also by David Dabydeen

Poetry:
Turner
Coolie Odyssey

Fiction:
The Intended
Disappearance
The Counting House
A Harlot's Progress
Our Lady of Demerara
Molly and the Muslim Stick
Johnson's Dictionary (forthcoming)

Non-fiction:
Hogarth's Blacks: Images of Blacks in Eighteenth Century English Art
Hogarth, Walpole and Commercial Britain
Paks Britannica

SLAVE SONG

DAVID DABYDEEN

PEEPAL TREE

First published in Great Britain in 1984
by Dangaroo Press

This edition published in 2005
Reprinted in 2012
by Peepal Tree Press Ltd
17 King's Avenue
Leeds LS6 1QS
UK

ISBN 9781845230043

Supported using public funding by
ARTS COUNCIL
ENGLAND

For Anna Rutherford

CONTENTS

INTRODUCTION

It is the land of El Dorado, the country of the Golden City of the Prince of Manoa ... to Raleigh anyway who dreamt of setting up an Elizabethan Empire in Guiana. The poetic imagination was kindled, issuing in a splendour of images. 'A region of Guiana all good and bounty,' Falstaff described his Mistress Page. Milton, in *Paradise Lost,* wrote of 'unspoilt Guiana whose Great City Geryon's Sons call El Dorado'. In the 18th century, Guiana lost ground to China, Brazil, Tahiti and the South Sea Islands but came back brilliantly with Hudson's *Green Mansions* and Conan Doyle's *The Lost World,* both set in its hinterlands.

Alas, these days the English are literally down to earth bothering only with the extraction of bauxite for their tin cans and the business of sugar refining for their toffees ... the Prince of Manoa is now the brand-name of a box of chocolates.

But to do a Crabbe-like hatchet-job on Raleigh is beside the point for his dream *is* an inexpressibly poignant thing. We are, in literature anyway, creatures of peasant flesh squelching through mud and cane-field, bearing about us the stench of fish and fresh blood. In the moment of our rawness there is recoil, the cry for transfiguration is heard which to the Guyanese is the cry for 'whiteness', for the spiritual qualities of Raleigh's Elizabethan Empire. 'England' is our Utopia, an ironic reversal, for Raleigh was looking away from the 'squalor' of his homeland to the imagined purity of ours whereas we are now reacting against our 'sordid' environment and looking to 'England' as Heaven. All is a criss-cross of illusions, a trading in skins and ideals.

I have only sketched the skeleton of things for the situation is more complex, never a black and white one. Our desire for 'whiteness' is as spiritual as it is banal. On one level it is a craving for mind and soul – the 'savage' wants civilization of the Renaissance kind; on a baser level what he wants is the 'civilization' of cars and fridges – a mere materialist greed. Ironically the white utopianists in English history and literature – Warton, Pratt, Berkeley, Day and others – were reacting against the luxuries and material excesses of their 'civilization' and finding true 'civilization' in the foreign lands. On other levels the cry for 'whiteness' is a sexual appetite. 18th Century white idealization of the Female Noble Savage is invariably bound up with a desire for sexual experience with her, often of a degrading kind, as Fairchild revealed in a study of such literature: sex with the Black meant a liberation from the restraints of civilized behaviour and codes of politeness – that is, a release from the white man's burden of having to appear decent. The white man desired the freedom to indulge in a bestial, fevered sensuality – in what Defoe in the 18th Century described as 'unspeakable acts of copulation'; in what Lawrence in the 20th Century described as the 'hot, fecund darkness of the African body'. The fantasy of dominance, bondage and sado-masochism, of sensual corruption and disintegration, could be enacted upon the submissive, inferior black female. Hence Jonathan Corncob is initiated into the sensual, tropical degradation of taking a 'Negress' straight from the cane-fields, hot, dirty and drenched in rank sweat. If black flesh was bewitching, the same fascination is found for the white woman, from the native point of view – except that this latter lust is an inverse to the former, describable in terms of inspiration, aspiration, assimilation into a superior scheme of things. The poems in this volume (a jumble of fact and myth, past and present) are largely concerned with an exploration of the erotic energies of the colonial experience, ranging from a corrosive to a lyrical sexuality. Even the appetite for sadistic sexual possession is life giving, the strange, vivid fruit of racial conquest and racial hatred. I say a 'jumble of fact and myth' because my purpose is not to provide a sociologically 'accurate' transcript of 'reality' but rather an *imaginative* rendition and reconstruction, a private fantasy.

Most Guyanese are peasant labourers and the majority of these work in Sugar Estates, all owned until recently by a British company, Bookers. Ironically, Bookers are involved in English literature (the Booker Prize) as well as in the real exploitation of literature's Noble Savage. They foster the illusion whilst at the same time profiting from the reality.

The peasants work in what are called 'creole gangs' of men and women. The men cut the cane, this being the most laborious part of the sugar and rum business. Guyana, from the cane plant, produces some of the finest rums in the world, as Western connoisseurs of the stuff will admit. The workers themselves can hardly afford to buy the bottles that

10

grace the cabinets of foreigners, and they distill their own, a highly illegal operation for it deprives the Government of revenues from the sale of proper rum. The product of the back-yard stills is called 'bush-rum'. Its potency is notorious, causing madness, blindness and sexual impotence if consumed in sufficient quantities – and it is! Bush rum is their drug and their destroyer: in view of the fact that there is nothing else to do after coming home from work in the fields, the men don't mind what its effects are, so long as it gets them merry as well. The women do: severe and habitual wife-beating is a common feature of village life, part of the culture almost, and a large percentage of murders is done under the influence of bush rum. It is therefore an absurd situation: men work, cutting cane and the fruit of their labour, bush rum, is what kills them. It is all suicidal. Why be born in the first place? – but even that was not by choice.

The peasant women have their day, the sexes balance out. Before long, the power of the men has waned considerably due to hard work and hard drinking and the women take over almost completely. They take over the children and control of all business pertaining to the household. The men are physically at an end but the women are still sexually alive, especially in the period of menopause. The male inadequacy creates enormous tensions in the household especially when adultery is an unthinkable step due to cultural and religious conditioning; due too to the quick currency of gossip in a village community. Emotions are pent-up therefore and frustration, instead of being assuaged outside the home, say, in an extra-marital relationship, is directed at the husband. The womb yearns, like Lorca's Yerma's, a battle rages until old age cools all fires, and death. The children are inevitably caught up in the conflict: they take the side of the mother, influenced by memories of the brutal hand of the father. As they grow up, they can develop an extremely scornful attitude to the father. In the end he is a solitary, beaten figure, an outcast in his own home, with nothing but alcohol to manage his loneliness.

Apart from the drinking of bush rum the business of cutting cane is sordid in itself. There are the dangers of poisonous snakes in the canefields and the inevitable slipping of the cutlass that gashes some part of the anatomy, but besides these minor matters is the sheer physical hardness of the work. It saps all strength, for not only does one have to cut the cane, one has to fetch it as well to punts located in the canal which skirts the field and leads off to the factory. The canecutter, naked to the waist in the tropical heat, chops away all day with his cutlass and towards sunset he separates the cane he has cut down into bundles and takes these to be weighed and then dumped into the punts. Each bundle might weigh up to 100 pounds and he walks to and fro fetching his cane to the punts which might be a quarter of a mile away. He may have to make as many as ten trips to convey all the bundles. It's not a pleasant evening's walk.

If the men are involved in one part of the field chopping down cane, the women may be planting and manuring it in another. The women were also employed in clearing trenches, fetching bagasse, weeding fields, and other such tasks. Their experience of the plantation field was as brutal as that of the men – George Pinckard' s 19th Century survey of the West Indies included this passage on the work of the women:

> At one spot, in the course of our ride, we had our attention arrested by observing a party of four, almost naked, females working in a cane field. Curiosity would not allow us to pass on without devoting to them a moment of particular regard. We, therefore, went a little *off* the road to approach them nearer; when we found that they were labouring with the hoe, to dig, or cut up the ground, preparatory to the planting of sugar; and that a stout robust looking man, apparently white, was following them, holding a whip at their backs.

The ritual of cutting and planting then differs from the sower and his seeds in the pre-Christian violence of the operation. Canecutting is a savage ceremony, cutlass slashing away relentlessly at bamboo-hard body of cane; planting is equally vicious, a repeated stabbing into the soil. There is no tenderness or respect for the earth. Male and female are involved in one continuous and conflicting ritual of cutting and planting. Needless to say the conflict continues after work, at home.

This brings us finally to the 'vulgarity' of the language. It is the vulgarity of the people, the vulgarity of their way of life. There is little grace, peace, politeness in their lives, only a lot of cane. If cane dominates life, it also dominates death. If a Guyanese peasant dies and one inquires of his family or friends the cause of death, the invariable answer is 'sugar in the blood'. All non-visible fatal illnesses, whether it be in reality cancer or coronary disease or whatever, are attributed to this mysterious 'sugar in the blood' – meaning diabetes.

The language is angry, crude, energetic. The canecutter chopping away at the crops bursts out in a spate of obscene words, a natural gush from the gut, like fresh faeces. It's hard to put two words together in Creole without swearing. Words are spat out from the mouth like live squibs, not pronounced with elocution. English diction is cut up and this adds to the abruptness of the language: 'what' for instance becomes 'wha' (as in 'whack') the splintering making the language more barbaric. Soft vowel sounds are habitually converted: the English tend to be polite in 'war' ('wor') whereas the Creole 'warre' produces the appropriate snarling sound; 'scorn' becomes 'scaan', 'mortar', 'mata', 'water', 'wata', etcetera. To list the various ways in which English is converted into Creole, with various effects, is inappropriate here and is the business of the philologist, except to say that the speed of Creole speech, the accent with which it is pronounced and the various Asian and African words mixed into it would make it foreign to an Englishman's ear. Writing it down on paper minimizes the difficulties and it becomes quite readable. However the language is primarily oral and the following pieces are meant to be spoken aloud, not read silently, for the tone of them to come through, not merely the abstracted meaning. In an oral language tone creates meaning. Creole is intensely kinetic, and gestures naturally and spontaneously accompany oral delivery.

Another feature of the language is its brokeness, no doubt reflecting the brokeness and suffering of its original users – African slaves and East Indian indentured labourers. Its potential as a naturally tragic language is there, there in its brokeness and rawness which is like the rawness of a wound. If one has learnt and used Queen's English for some years, the return to Creole is painful, almost nauseous for the language is uncomfortably raw, as I said, like a wound. One has to shed one's protective sheath of abstracts and let the tongue move freely in blood again. One has to get accustomed to the unsheathing of the tongue and the contact with raw matter.

In the following pieces I have attempted to exploit the brutality of the language, relating it to the brutality of its users. In *Song of the Creole Gang Women,* the contraction of words like 'work' into 'wuk' (line 1) is typical of the intensity of the Creole language – like the word 'juk' (line 7) which conveys perfectly the sensation of being violently pierced, or the word 'caad' for 'cord' (line 28), the hardening of the sound enacting the sensation of being savagely strapped. The song is made harsh in tone by the monosyllabic starkness of words and by their crude and ruthless rhyming – 'maan ... waan ... baan ... faan ... haan ... saang'. But the language is also capable of a lyrical effect, a sensuous and gentle effect:

> Leh we go sit dung riverside, dip, dodo, die,
> Shade deep in cool deh.

The English fails where the Creole succeeds, particularly in the impossible translation of 'dodo' as 'sleep' for the word 'dodo' means more than sleep and is inseparable from a specific action – the comforting of a child when it is crying by kissing it or patting it until it is quietened and at rest. In addition the simple monosyllables are not crude; they slide into each other – 'dip ... die ... deep ... deh' – a fluidity achieved not by the alliteration but by a simple variation of vowel sounds. The fluid rhythm is further enhanced by simple rhymes like 'leh' and 'deh' ('let' and 'there').

I have also retained the full vulgarity of the language for it is a profound element in Guyanese life: for instance, in *The Canecutters' Song,* I wanted to show the Creole mind straining and struggling after concepts of beauty and purity (imaged in the White Woman), but held back by its crude, physical vocabulary. The canecutter aspires to lyrical experience and expression but cannot escape his condition of squalor nor the crude diction that such a condition generates. So to describe her beauty he struggles to transform vulgar words and concepts into lyrical ones, the result being both poignant and funny: 'the hibiscus flowers in your panties, wet and soft and white' or 'your puss-mouth (i.e. vagina) glows, meshed with light, the sun seeds and sprouts there' (he is trying here to describe the beautiful and fascinating aspect of her blondness, a colour that is strange to his sexual environment, making her unearthly). He has no 'poetical' words because his experience of life under colonialist rule was never 'poetical'. The craving for 'transfiguration' (or 'abstraction') mentioned earlier is constantly frustrated. He cannot escape his words, cannot escape the mud.

The potentiality for literature is very great indeed, for the language, if mastered, is capable of expressing the full experience of its users which is a very deep one, deep in suffering, cruelty, drunken merriment and tenderness. The brief moments of tenderness, usually in sexual courtship or old age, appear all the more profound and memorable because of the norm of pain. It is surprising therefore that very little Creole poetry exists – a handful of folk-songs mostly. With notable exceptions the writers that exist are educated in Western Culture and write like Westerners; or else they write tourist poetry about famous 'beauty-spots' in Guyana, like the Kaiteur Waterfalls; or else they are mere lackeys to the present régime, churning out political stuff, exhorting the workers to produce more for less pay. It's all a fervently stupid patriotism when what is needed is true 'patriotism', that is a recognition and expression of the uniqueness of the people, the particularity of their being.

SONG OF THE CREOLE GANG WOMEN

1st Woman

Wuk, nuttin bu wuk
Maan noon an night nuttin bu wuk
Booker own me patacake
Booker own me pickni.
Pain, nuttin bu pain
Waan million tous'ne acre cane.
O since me baan – juk! juk! juk! juk! juk!
So sun in me eye like taan
So Booker saach deep in me flesh
Kase Booker own me rass
An Booker own me cutlass –
Bu me dun cuss ... Gaad leh me na cuss no mo!

Caan in me finga, caan in me foot-battam,,.

Chorus

Dosay an mittae, dosay an mittae,
Booker put e mout on me like pirae.

2nd Woman

Kiss-kiss-kidee! Kiss-kiss-kiss-kideee!
So wind a howl from de haat o bush
Like bird mesh, tear up on twig.
Hear, hear how e'ya cry, cry, how e'ya bleed on de air,
An bruk up over bud aweh hooman, sickle in haan,
Sweep an sway all day to e saang
Babee strap like burden to we back.
Kiss-kiss-kidee! Kiss-kiss-kiss-kideee!

Chorus

Dutty-skin, distress, shake aff we babee
When we reach wataside shake aff we patakee.

3rd Woman

Is true everyting stall, gape, bleed,
Like crappau foot squash jess as e'ya leap?

4th Woman

Everyting tie up, haat, lung, liva, an who go loose me caad? –
Shaap, straight, sudden like pimpla, cut free
An belly buss out like blood-flow a shriek?
Or who saaf haan, saaf-flesh finga?
Or who go paste e mout on me wound, lick, heal, like starapple suck?

5th Woman

Look a de sun how e fix in de sky like taskmasta eye,
A de coconut-tree dat watch over we like overseer
Treaten fo spill e load on we maiden head...
Me tust, dust an vinega choke me mout, sweat leak over me like
      gutta-wata
Heat a hatch louse in me hair...

Chorus

Leh we go sit dung riverside, dip, dodo, die –
Shade deep in cool deh.

(They move off, repeating these lines with mournful voices, that
gradually fade out. A deep silence.)

FOR MALA

1st Voice

Yesterday deh pull out young girl from de river tangle-
Up in de net in de fish, bloat, bubby bite-
Up, teet-mark in she troat an tigh:
Was na pirae.

2nd Voice

When deh bin done sport wid she, deh shove bruk-
Top bottle up she front jess fo fun, fo see she squirm
An hear she halla fo Gaad, fo she Muma halla.
She name bin call Mala.

1st Voice

Yesterday she womb bin live an stirrin wid clean, bright blood
Like starapple inside, full-flesh when yu squash it open
An all de ripe juice run dung yu finga, dung yu arm an troat.
Now she hollow, now she float.

2nd Voice

Mangoose run aff in de night, yolk a drip from e mout-kana.

1st Voice

Somebady juta Gaad holy fruit so man can't taste she
        sweetness no mo!
Petals o pus she womb put out, dry sticks fo blossom
Under de earth wheh she lie wid she eye open an she mout dumb.

2nd Voice

Pumpkin dat feed hungry mout now stuff dem guts wid fire.
Five-finga piece by piece drap dung from de sky an bleed in
     de grass –
Mala! Mala! wheh yu deh gal? wheh yu lass?

1st Voice

Gyden na go bear fruit!
Cow na go drap each year!
Wife na go grow big wid belly!
Snake go bite yu foot in savannah!
Alligita go eat yu sheep when dem crass wata!
Hear me cuss like malabunta in yu ear!

2nd Voice

Blackman go pung mata, na mattie head,
Feed dem pickni wid fufu, na mattie flesh,
Coolie grind massala, na mattie bone, stir dhall, na blood.
De air go fill wid curry-smell an roast cassava
Puri an pepperpot
An sitar an steelband go sound wheh gunfire bin a deh.
Lil pickni go laan plant wara-seed na pelt each odda in de
     street wid dem,
An when people kill, dem kill only cackroach, centipede, masquita...
Hear me dream like birdsaang in yu ear!

GUYANA PASTORAL

Under de tambrin tree wheh de moon na glow,
Laang, laang, laang, she lay, laang, laang
She cry, but de wind na blow
An dem wraang an straang
An dem wuk an dem bruk till fowlcack-crow.
Who see who hear when she belly buss, when she mout
        splash blood?

Only de jumbie umbrella dat poke up e white eye from de mud.

Under de tambrin tree wheh de sun na shine
Dem tek up spade, dem dig deep hole, dem hide she from deh mine.
She puppa look bush, how he hack, how he halla!
She mumma call priest, kill calf, pray Krishna, Christ, Allah!
Nine mont since dem saach an dem shout, East, West, Naat, Sout.
Who know wheh she lass, who know wheh fuh fine?

Only de cush-cush ants dat lay dem white egg in she mout.

THE SERVANTS' SONG

White hooman haad like hassa-bone stick in yu gum
Cassava pelt from she eye when she stare an scaan yu,
Dress-up in silk day time, prappa scunt in she silva slippa,
Everyday ting wraang wid she how she fuss
Is like bitch in heat how she yap an spit an scratch an cuss –
'Yu fine me gold ring yet wha me lass?'
'No Missie ... yes Missie ... yes Missie ... no Missie' an yu
        bow till yu neck turn rubba
'Well fine am, fine am, fine am leh me see!
Else me go whip all ayuh nigga tief-man!
Gwan, gwan, gwan! Haak-tuh!'
So we run
An we saach
Wid cutlass
Wid taach
In bush
In backdam
In gyden
In yaad
Till we bruk-up
Till we maad.
Gaad-O-Laad!
We saach kitchen, hall-kana in de house
We saach we hair like we comb fo louse.
Trow way de curry an look in de pot
Trow way de baby an look in de cot
Bu no ring deh!
O me mama, how me friken wha Missie go seh!
Wha we go do? We wring we haan
Saary-saary we bin baan –
Till Peta, chupit in e ead since e bin young baai when e fall
        dung coconut tree –
Man chase am, hooman scaan am, call dem husband 'Peta'
        when dem a cuss –

Britannia and the Natives

Dis maad-rass, maga-baai seh,
'Leh we go look in duck-battie, me geh mind da ring deh-deh
All night me studyation dis ting an me know e deh-deh.'
He run fowl-pen, pick out waan by chance
Raise up e fedda, skin e leg an peep –
How aweh laugh!
Duck na know wha do am, duck halla, duck leggo waan shit –
An ring come out – if yu see leap!
If yu see dance!
All bady hug up a maad baai an shake e haan
Hooman squeeze up e lolo how dem so happy!
An all bady seh, 'Aweh use to mock yu Peta, now aweh go laan.'
Den we wash ring, tek am gi Missie
She put am on she finga
Bu we na tell she wheh we fine am.
An when she show aff an she kiss she ring she na know why
        all aweh laugh so loud
She beg we foh tell till she beat we, bribe we, but leh she kiss
        we rass first!

A piece of sugar cane

THE CANECUTTERS' SONG

(The slow throbbing of a drum at long intervals, growing louder and quicker as the song proceeds, then breaking into a wild uncontrolled beating at the last few lines of the song. The men move slowly around the solitary canecutter with slight dance gestures that also intensify gradually.)

Canecutter

White hooman walk tru de field fo watch we canecutta,
Tall, straight, straang-limb,
Hair sprinkle in de wind like gold-duss,
Lang lace frack loose on she bady like bamboo-flag,
An flesh mo dan hibiscus early maan, white an saaf an wet
Flowering in she panty.
O Shanti! Shanti! Shanti!
Wash dis dutty-skin in yu dew
Wipe am clean on yu saaf white petal!
O Shanti! Shanti! Shanti! —
So me spirit call, so e halla foh yu
When me peep out at yu tween cane-stalk, strain me nose
     foh ketch yu scent
Bram-bram bram-bram beat me haat till me friken yu go hear —
Bu daylight separate me an yu, an dis mud on me haan
Dis sweat from me face, dis rag on me back...
Yu puss-mouth glow, mesh wid light, sun a seed an sprout deh
Me too black fo come deh —
Bu when night come how me dream...
Dat yu womb lie like starapple buss open in de mud
An how me hold yu dung, wine up yu waiss
Draw blood from yu patacake, daub am all over yu face
Till yu dutty like me an yu halla
Like when cutlass slip an slice me leg, an yu shake
Like when snake twist rung me foot, when we cut cane...

So me dream
When night come
An masquita wake up from de bush,
Malabunta move.

Chorus

Baai yu ever dream she drawsie-down!
Baai yu ever wuk she wid yu tongue!
Baai yu ever taste she pokey
Saaf an drippy like baigan-chokey!

The Execution and Breaking on the Rack.

SLAVE SONG

Tie me haan up.
Juk out me eye.
Haal me teet out
So me na go bite.
Put chain rung me neck.
Lash me foot tight.
Set yu daag fo gyaad
Maan till nite –

Bu yu caan stap me cack floodin in de goldmine
Caan stap me cack splashin in de sunshine!

Whip me till me bleed
Till me beg.
Tell me how me hanimal
African orang-utan
Tell mc how me cannibal
Fit fo slata fit fo hang.
Slice waan lip out
Waan ear an waan leg –

Bu yu caan stap me cack dippin in de honeypot
Drippin at de tip an happy as a hottentot!

Look how e'ya leap from bush to bush like a black crappau
Seeking out a watahole,
Blind by de sunflare, tongue like a dussbowl –
See how e'ya sip laang an full an slow!
Till e swell an heavy, stubban, chupit, full o sleep
Like camoudie swalla calf an stretch out in de grass, content,
Full o peace...
Hibiscus bloom, a cool breeze blow
An from a hill a wataflow
Canary singin saaf an low...

Is so when yu dun dream she pink tit,
Totempole she puss,
Leff yu teetmark like a tattoo in she troat!

She gi me taat
She gi me wife
So tear out me liver
Or stake me haat
Me still gat life!

LOVE SONG

Moon-eye
Blue like blue-saki wing,
Moon-eye, all maan in me mine...

Black man cover wid estate ash
E ead haad an dry like calabash,
Dut in e nose-hole, in e ear-hole,
Dut in e soul, in e battie-hole.

All
day
sun
bun
tongue
bun
all
day
troat
cut
haat
hut
wuk na dun, na dun, na dun!
Hack! Hack! Hack! Hack!
Cutlass slip an cut me cack!

Tank Gaad six a'clack!
Me go home
An me go bade
An me go comb
An me go rock
In hammock
Cassava, pepperpot,
Drink some rum an coconut!

... When me soul saaf an me eye wet
An de breeze blow an me eye shet
An de bakle na ga mo rum
Den leh yuh come
An tek me wey, wheh
Chain na deh, wheh
Cane na deh.
Leh yuh come wid milk in yuh breast an yuh white troat bare
Wid bangle on yuh haan an bell rung yuh waiss
Leh yuh come wid oil an perfume an lace...

Moon-eye
Blue like blue-saki wing,
Silk frack tumble an splash on me face like wata-fall
An yuh dance an yuh call
In de night.

ELEGY

So yu lean over landing, early cole maaning
Old man, yu sick? Is wha do yu? Wha wraang?
An yu haan weak, tremble, an yu mout move
Bu word na deh, an yu eye stare out at de field, laang, laang,
Bu yu na see calf stir an struggle foh suck
An yu na hear high from jamoon tree bluesaki saang –
Is old yu old ... is dah wha mek ...

Snakeneck, Fisheye, Badman, Rich'ed,
Young yesterday, all a dem baais, Tiefman, Blackbattie, Goose,
Late late in de night ayuh drink rum ayuh beat drum,
Roast crab, curass, tell jumbie story till maaning come...
Is wheh dem deh? All lay up dem net, all put dung dem
        cutlass, all let dem sheep loose,
All dead!
An Jasmattie beating claat on de riverbank – tump! tump!
        tump! tump!
How she haan straang an she back straight an she bubby
        sweet sapadilla-brung!
Yu memba when yu fuss see she how yu troat lump?
How she young bady leap, leak blood, when yu roll she pun
        de grung? ...

All dem slingshat buss, all dem fence bruk-
Dung, so jackass graze in dem vegetable gyaaden, bird a peck,
Fireside crack, an battamhouse, an puckni na blow, bellnay
        na wuk –
An is wha mek....?

NIGHTMARE

Bruk dung de door!
Waan gang sweat-stink nigga
Drag she aff she bed
Wuk pun she
Crack she head
Gi she jigga
Tween she leg!

Dem chase she backdam:
Waan gang cane-stiff cack
Buss she tail till she blue an black
Till she crawl tru de mud an she bawl an she beg.

Dem haul she canal-bank like bush-haag
Cut she troat over de dark surging wata
When dem dun suck dem raise dem red mout to de moon
An mek saang,

Deep in de night when crappau call an cush-cush
Crawl dung hole, lay dem egg in de earth
When camoudie curl rung calf dat just drap
An black bat flap-flap-flap tru de bush...

Wet she awake, cuss de daybreak!

A Rebel Negro.

MEN AND WOMEN

So me saary.
Bu when yu grow old an yu voice weak an yu mout dribble
An yu foot-battam crack,
Is too late
Foh seh saary.

Bu me still saary.

Kase me drink rum an beat yu
Young saaf wet-eye face.
Kase me gi yu big belly year after year
Nine pickni foh feed, an me run way wid sweet-hooman
Sport all me inheritance whore-house.
Kase yu wuk in de field maaning till night, bruise-
Up yu small haan an yu skin peel in de sun.
Kase when yu sit dung an roll roti, or rock baby in hammock,
Yu na sing glad-glad like odda hooman
How yu mout sour like aachar.

Me come back now, bu now yu old
An yu na know me
How yu mind weak
An yu eye dull.
Bu blood stir in me bady still when me look pun yu,
Like laang-time, when yu was me midnight bride,
Bright, fresh, hopeful, an me lay yu dung dunlopilla bed –
Downstairs dem a beat drum, dem a sing love saang, dem a
        dance in de firelight! ...

An me saary bad!

FOR MA

Roll roti! roll roti! roll roti! roll roti!
Curry cookin in de karahee
Bora boilin wid de bagee
Woodsmoke sweet in me nose like agarbattee –
Ayuh wake up wake up ayuh pickni wake up ayuh man
Wid de sunshine in yu eye an de river a flow
An brung doves burstin from de trees an de kiskidees
An de whole savannah swimmin green an a glow!

Wata foh fetch battam-house foh daub fresh bucket foh
        mend clothes foh beat
Wake up ayuh pickni wuk na dun wuk foh duh
Cutlass foh shaap wood foh chap fence foh build dat bull
        bruk dung
Is wha da maan a stretch e haan an yaan foh!
Hear a cow baal in de yaad how dem swell wid milk-fraff
Goat a groan dem want go graze an sheep a caff-caff –
Ayuh wake up wake up time na deh foh cry time na deh foh laff
Hen a lay an cow a drap time na deh foh stap!

SLAVEWOMAN'S SONG

Ya howl –
Hear how ya howl –
Tell me wha ya howl foh
Tell me noh?
Pickni?
Dem tek pickni way?
Wha dem do wid pickni
Mek yu knaack yu head wid stone
Bite yu haan like daag-bone?

Is husban mek yu halla gal?
Wha dem do wid maan
Mek yu daub yu face wid cow dung
Juk yu eye an chap yu tongue?
Dem trow am Demerara, feed am alligata?

Muma? Pupa? Africa?
Belly big wid Massa?

Ya howl –
Hear how ya howl –
Tell me wha ya howl foh
Tell me noh?

A Female Negro Slave with a Weight Chained to her Ankle.

BROWN SKIN GIRL

Gwan, gwan America brung skin gyal,
Meet white maan.
Yu go laan
Taak prappa, dress, drive car,
Hold knike an faak in yu haan:
De mud, de canal, de canefield gaan
An me wid ricebowl drinkin mar
Me wid ricebowl tinkin far.

Gwan, gwan America brung skin gyal,
Mek money, mek pickni,
Move smood, stand tall:
Cackroach, kreketeh,
Maskita na deh-deh
Fo bruk yu life fo mek yu crawl,
An me wid fishnet waitin tide
Dreams like bleedin deep inside.

A Surinam Planter in his Morning Dress.

TWO CULTURES

'Hear how a baai a taak
Like BBC!
Look how a baai a waak
Like white maan,
Caak-hat pun he head, wrist-watch pun he haan!
Yu dadee na Dabydeen, plant gyaden near Blackbush Pass?
He na cut wid sickle an dig wid faak?
He na sell maaket, plantain an caan?
An a who pickni yu rass?
Well me never see story like dis since me baan!

E bin Inglan two maaning, illegal,
Eye-up waan-two white hooman,
Bu is wha dem sweet watalily seed
Go want do wid hungrybelly Blackbush weed
Like yu, how yu teet yella like dhall
An yu tongue black like casrip!
Dem should a spit, vamit pun yu, beat yu rass wid whip!
Is lungara like yu spoil dem good white people country,
Choke an rab, bruk-an-enta, tief dem people prapaty!

So yu tink yu can come hey an play big-shat,
Fill we eye wid cigarette, iceapple an all dat?
Aweh po country people bu aweh ga pride:
Jess touch me gyal-pickni, me go buss yu back-side.'

SONG OF THE CREOLE GANG WOMEN

The *Song of the Creole Gang Women* is their cry against the sun and against white society; it is also the cry of sexual frustration and the cry for sexual relief. The image of the 'crappau' (a native frog) being squashed by the foot just as it is about to leap is central in conveying this, and in terms of Guyanese life it is an immediate and recognisable image: in the frog season, it is impossible to walk the land without stamping down upon a frog, a very unpleasant and bloody experience. The stench of dead frogs is everywhere, it rankles in the consciousness.

The women bind their waists and abdomens tightly, with cords ('caad') – that is, stripped bark of the troolie tree or banana leaves. This is to prevent strains and belly-aches by keeping the intestines in place for they are continually bending and raising themselves in the process of planting cane. The cords are a sort of makeshift corset. Abdominal pains afflict them terribly in old age if they do not tie up their bellies when they are young and they believe that the power to bear children is also affected without the precaution of 'caad'. 'Everything tied up, heart, lung, liver, and who will loose my cords?' – it is the constant craving and complaint of peasant women.

The squashed crappau and the bandaged, almost mummified women are identified in the song as are their babies strapped on to their backs, usually in a sort of rice-bag sack, their little tiny heads peeping out comically – and pathetically – at the world of cane and at all the strange activity of strange extra-maternal forms.

The female cry is for the release of the womb – 'the belly bursts out like blood-flow shrieking.' (The connotation is of a woman's menstrual flow as a sign of fertility.) This gush differs from the intestinal spill of the squashed frog in that it is vital. The fourth Woman fantasizes about such release, the womb cut open savagely by a 'pimpla'. The 'pimpla' is a gigantic white thorn, a menace to the countryside of Guyana. The use of the 'pimpla' image indicates that although the white man is the menace and subject of complaint (the first Woman cries that 'Booker' cuts into her flesh like a thorn –'taan'), the women are still fascinated by him: they have a touch of masochism in them and the intensity of their language betrays a surreptitious savouring of their pain. They are both fascinated and repelled by his tyranny as by the squashed crappau which they want to become, yet are sickened by. All this does not however detract from the pity felt for their condition of suffering.

The Chorus sings of the waterside: during their break for lunch the women leave the fields to sit down by the riverside or canal-bank. There they unshackle their babies, drop their cutlasses, loosen their clothes to let the breezes in and bathe their limbs, washing off the cane stains and cane smell. To stumble upon them is like coming upon victims of rape – such is the chaos of attitudes, and the abandon of bodies, and the ache. Piranha ('pirae' – flesh-eating fish) frequent such waters, hence the meaning of their first song:

> Dosay and mittae, dosay and mittae
> Booker puts his mouth on me like pirae

Dosay and mittae are sweet foods made from cane sugar; the image is of the fish attracted to sweetened flesh, to the women with their sugar-cane aroma which washes off in the water. They are fascinated and horrified by the danger – the fish would mutilate their flesh as they wished their wombs to be by the 'pimpla', and as the frog is. The second choric song carries the desire for self-destruction further. They sing of throwing off their babies when they reach the waterside and also of 'shaking off their patacakes' (female sexual parts). The riverside means physical liberation, release from their 'cords', their children and their sexuality. It is a violent death-desire but by the final choric song the thought of suicide loses its hysteria and becomes lyrical, as if what was imagined is now enacted, made actual.

Line 16: The Kiskadee is a tropical tyrant-bird named after its shrill call: 'Kiss-kiss-kidee', 'kiss-kiss-kiss-kidee'.

Line 32: The Starapple is the sweetest and strangest of Guyanese fruits. When ripe it has a dark purple skin; inside its flesh is the texture of human flesh, raw and running with juice, flesh that like the skin is of a rich, deep purple. The juice literally stains the lips and the flesh pastes on to the mouth and tongue since it oozes a sticky white liquid when sucked. In the song it is used with oral-sexual implications.

TRANSLATION:

Work, nothing but work/ Morning noon and night nothing but work/
Booker owns my cunt/ Booker owns my children/ Pain, nothing but
pain/ One million thousand acres cane/ O since I was born – stab! stab!
stab! stab! stab!/ So sun in my eye like thorn/ So Booker searches deep
in my flesh/ Because Booker owns my arse/ And Booker owns my
cutlass/ But I'm done with cursing, God let me not curse any more/
Corn in my finger, corn in my foot-bottom.

Dosay and mittae, dosay and mittae/ Booker puts his mouth on me like
piranha.

Kiss-kiss-kidee/ Kiss-kiss-kiss-kideee!/ So wind howls from the heart of
bush/ Like a bird meshed, torn upon twigs/ Hear how it cries, cries, how
it bleeds on the air/ And broken over buds we women, sickles in hand/
Sweep and sway all day to its song/ Babies strapped like burdens to our
backs/ Kiss-kiss-kidee/ Kiss-kiss-kiss-kideee!

Dirty-skin, distressed, shake off our babies/ When we reach waterside
shake off our wombs.

Is it true everything stalls, gapes, bleeds/ Like frog foot squashes just as
it is about to leap?

Everything tied up, heart, lung, liver, and who will loose my cords?/
Sharp, straight, sudden, like pimpla, cut them free/ And belly bursts out
like blood-flow shrieking?/ Or whose soft hand, soft-fleshed finger?/ Or
who will paste his mouth on my wound, lick, heal, like starapple suck?

Look at the sun how it's fixed in the sky like a taskmaster's eye/ At the
coconut-trees that watch over us like an overseer/ Threatening to spill
his load on our maiden heads.../ I'm thirsty, dust and vinegar choke my
mouth, sweat leaks over me like gutter-water/ Heat hatches lice in my
hair.

Let's go sit down riverside, dip, sleep, die/ Shade deep in cool there.

For Mala is about the main heritage of the Colonial Era, which is racial conflict. When the Negro slaves were freed, East Indian indentured labourers were brought in to replace them in the sugar estates, at the middle and end of the nineteenth century. The two races were kept apart and the natural suspicion that exists between any two races or peoples was surcharged in the 'Divide and Rule' policy.

In 1964, a few years before independence, racial clashes took place on an unprecedented scale and a free-for-all slaughter occurred. The high point of barbarity, and the blackest episode of the year occurred at Wismar, a predominantly Negro village at the edge of the Demerara River where in the space of a few hours hundreds of East Indian residents were attacked. The men and children were locked up in their houses which were then set afire. The women and young girls were raped, mutilated and then dumped into the river to die. It was collective violence and the collective realization of sexual fantasy on a frightening scale – the 'savages' had become *real* savages and certainly not noble.

Line 13: The favourite diet of the mongoose is chicken's eggs, and chickens themselves.

Line 14: To 'juta' is a Hindu word meaning to spoil food by eating it firstly before its proper time, and secondly with dirty hand or tongue. No English translation is really possible. In the song it refers to the rape of the young girl, Mala, taken before her time, i.e. before her womanhood and thus despoiled; also the bodily filth of the rapists.

'To juta God's holy fruit' is to the Hindu a great sin: what is set aside for God (in religious ceremonies) is sacrosanct and to eat it is a great violation.

Line 17: An East Indian is said to have stuffed explosives in a large pumpkin and placed it in a river launch. 24 people, most of them Negroes, were drowned or blown up.

Line 18: On March 27th, a Negro activist was found lying unconscious with seven of his fingers blown away.

Line 18: The 'Five-finger fruit' is the name of a Guyanese fig (here connected with the human fingers scattered abroad by explosives, and with the dismemberment, the piecing up and dispersal of Mala). The song is a series of images about food. Feeding is one of the most basic and urgent of peasant activities, sex and spilling blood being the others. Feeding, sex and bloodshed are made one in the song.

The rape and mutilation with a broken-neck bottle is something that actually happened to one of the victims of Wismar, so I'm told.

Line 26: Massala is an ingredient of curry; 'dhall' is 'lentil'.

Line 27: 'Fufu' is a favourite Negro food made by crushing plantains in a mortar ('mata') and adding various spices. The procedure of making the food is called 'punging mata' (pounding mortar). 'Pepperpot' and 'puri' (line 30) are Negro and Indian foods respectively.

Line 32: 'Wara-seed' is the hard, stony seed of the Awara fruit, used by the children to play marbles or as sling-weapons.

TRANSLATION:

Yesterday they pulled out a young girl from the river, tangled/ Up in the nets among the fish, bloated, breasts bitten/ All over, teeth marks in her throat and thigh./ It wasn't piranha.

When they had finished sporting with her, they shoved/ A broken bottle up her front just for the fun of seeing her squirm/ And hearing her cry for God, cry for her mother/ Her name was Mala.

Yesterday her womb was alive and stirring with clean, bright blood/ Like a starapple inside, full-fleshed when you squash it open/ And all its ripe juice runs down your fingers, down your arms and throat/ Now she's hollow, now she floats.

Mongoose runs off in the night, yolk dripping from the corner of his mouth.

Somebody has spoilt God's holy fruit and man will taste her sweetness no more/ Petals of pus her womb puts out, dry sticks for blossom/ Under the earth where she lies with her eyes open and her mouth dumb.

Pumpkin that fed hungry mouths now stuff their guts with fire/ Five-fingers piece by piece drop down from the sky, bleeds in the grass/ Mala! Mala! Where are you girl? Where are you lost?

Garden will not bear fruit!/ Cow will not drop calves each year!/ Wife will not swell with child!/ Snake will bite your foot in the savannah!/ Alligator will eat your sheep when they cross water!/ Hear my curse like wasps in your ear!

Blackman will pound mortar, not people's heads/ Feed their children with fufu, not people's flesh/ Coolie [i.e. the East Indian] will grind massala not people's bones, stir dhall not blood/ The air will fill with the scents of curry and roast cassava/ Puri and pepperpot/ And sitar and steelband will sound where gunfire was heard/ Little children will learn to plant wara-seeds not pelt each other with them./ And when people kill, it will be cockroach, centipede, mosquito .../ Hear my dream like birdsong in your ear/

GUYANA PASTORAL

The rape and murder of a young girl, told in hard, brutal rhythms, signify the violent aspect of Guyanese existence. The 'jumbie-umbrella' (types of white mushrooms that sprout overnight and are therefore thought of as ghostly things by the people; 'jumbie' means 'ghost') and 'cush-cush ants' convey the grotesque fecundity of natural life which participates in the process of violence, gaining strength by it. Nature itself (the tamarind tree's broad, dark cover; the moon; the wind) seems to conspire in this savagery.

TRANSLATION:

Under the tamarind tree where the moon doesn't glow/ Long, long, long she lay, long, long/ She cries but the wind doesn't blow/ And they're wrong and strong/ And they work her and they break her till fowlcock's crow/ Who sees, who hears when her belly bursts, when her mouth splashes blood?

Only the jumbie-umbrella that pokes up its white eye from the mud

Under the tamarind tree where the sun doesn't shine/ They take up spade, they dig deep hole, they hide her from their minds/ Her father searches the bush, how he hacks, how he's hoarse with calling!/ Her mother calls a priest, kills a calf, prays to Krishna, Christ, Allah!/ Nine months since they've searched and they've shouted, East, West, North, South/ Who knows where she's lost, and who knows where to find her?

Only the cush-cush ants that lay their white eggs in her mouth.

THE SERVANTS' SONG

The Servants' Song is an example of Guyanese peasant humour, simple and bawdy in a Chaucerian way but more crude. Vulgarity is as natural as a cow-pat, as indicated above. However, on a serious level, the poem does reveal some of the characteristics of village life. For instance Peter, the village idiot – he fell from a coconut-tree when he was young and damaged his brain, a not uncommon village accident – who is the saviour of the moment.

It tells too of the social situation of White Mistress and Black servants – the suffering of the latter, bullied and maltreated by the former in a show of triumph and superiority. In fact in the poem, the servants have the last laugh, as they sometimes did in real life; their resilience and satire are a sort of self-defence, necessary for survival under tyranny.

The hectic search for the ring and the subsequent discovery of it in the duck's anus is (metaphorically) indicative of some of the absurdity of life under Colonialist rule. Only the idiot Peter can cope with the situation; the sane peasants are perplexed.

The Servants' Song is founded upon a very simple Guyanese folk song:

> Missie lass [lost]
> Missie lass
> Missie lass she gold ring [her]
> O find am [it]
> Find am
> Find am leh me see! [let]

It is quite trivial for a folk song ('I've lost my ring! Find it!'), quite trivial, that is, until one tries to imagine the situation that produced it; until one tries to fill in the gaps that are unspoken, to clarify the hum and buzz of implication.

Line 1: 'Hassa' is a local fish, extremely hard and bony.

TRANSLATION:

White woman hard like fish-bone stuck in your gum/ Cassava pelts out from her eyes when she stares at us in scorn/ Dressed up in silk in the daytime, a proper cunt in her silver slippers/ Everyday there's something wrong with her, the way she fusses/ It's like a bitch in heat the way she yaps and spits and scratches and curses/ 'Have you found my gold ring yet that I lost?'/ 'No Missie … yes Missie … yes Missie … no Missie', and you bow until your neck becomes rubbery/ 'Well find it, find it, find it let me see!/ Or else I'll whip the lot of you nigger-thieves!/ Out, out, out!' (she spits after them)/ So we run/ and we search/ with cutlass/ with torch/ in bush/ in backdam/ in garden/ in yard/ till we're broken up/ till we're mad/ Lord God!/ We search in the kitchen, hall, all corners in the house/ We search our hair like we're combing for lice/ Throw away the curry and look in the pot/ Throw away the baby and look in the cot/ But there's no ring!/ O my mother, how I'm afraid of what Missie will say!/ What shall we do? We wring our hands/ Sorry-sorry we were born/ Till Peter, stupid in his head since he was a young boy when he fell down a coconut-tree/ Men shoo him away, women are scornful of him, call their husband 'Peter' when they are cursing/ This mad-arsed, emaciated boy says/ 'Let's go look up duck's backside, my mind tells me that the ring is there/ All night I thought and dreamt upon this thing and I just know it's there'/ He runs to the fowl-pen, picks out the nearest duck/ Raises up its feathers, parts its legs and peeps/ How we laughed!/ The duck didn't know what was happening, the duck screamed, the duck let loose a stream of shit/ And the ring came out — you should see how we leapt!/ And how we danced!/ Everybody hugged up this mad boy, shook his hands/ The women were so overjoyed that they fondled him all over/ And everybody said — 'We used to mock you Peter, now we'll learn.'/ Then we washed the ring, took it and gave it to Missie/ She put it on her finger/ But we didn't tell her where we found it/ And when she shows off and kisses her ring she wonders why we all burst out laughing/ She begs us to tell till she beats us, bribes us, but let her kiss our arse first!

THE CANECUTTERS' SONG

The hibiscus (line 5) is a lovely white-petalled flower of religious significance to Hindus since it is used in religious ceremonies: sung services of supplication and thanksgiving to Lord Krishna, with priest ('pandit') and congregation. Afterwards sweet foods, fruits and vegetable meals are shared out. These are totally vegetarian ceremonies, no flesh is to be brought in the proximity of priest and worshippers. Whilst this feasting is going on, a white flag is attached to a very tall, freshly-cut bamboo-stick (line 4) and this planted in the yard. A piece of gold, or gold dust (line 3) is wrapped in some cloth and this attached to the bamboo-pole – symbolic payment of Lord Krishna. For the whole community it is a day of joy and feasting, a rare and memorable occasion when there is abandon and plenty; there is dancing, singing, beating of drums late into the day.

The White Woman and such beautifully lyrical religious ceremonies are related in the first movement of the song. In the second movement the perversity of thought, the fantasy of rape is conveyed in non-vegetarian imagery; the *malabunta* (local wasp) and the *mosquito* feeding on flesh and blood, and the *snake*. The 'starapple' (line 19) marks the moment of change from the spiritual to the carnal and obscene, between the first and second movements – it is a fruit belonging to the table of religious festivity but, as explained previously, it is like raw flesh too. The 'baigan' (line 32), like the *starapple,* is of a deep purple colour. The English call it 'aubergine'. 'Baigan chokey' is a special preparation of the vegetable, roasting it so that its insides become semi-liquid, steaming and seedy. In the song, after the imagined rape, the canecutters use the 'baigan chokey' as an image of a spermatic mess. The image of feeding that runs through the song is on one level religious (the ceremonial feasting) and, on another, cannibalistic. Eating is a basic and most urgent feature of peasant life.

The name Shanti is a Hindu girl's name but it is also part of a religious phrase ('Om Shantih, Shantih, Shantih' – the end to an Upanishad) and like the starapple it is taken both ways by the canecutters – spiritually and sexually.

The song, starting idyllically, darkens, works up a passion, then culminates in a quick gush of obscenity; the sexual rhythm is paralleled by the rhythm of the drum-beat. The savage imagination of the canecutters is the correlate to the physical savagery of their work. Singing the song is therapeutic since it brings to the surface feelings that are buried under social pressures, and expresses what the cane-cutters cannot themselves verbalize because of their lack of command of words.

The song is poignant in so far as the canecutters realize that they can never achieve the sort of beauty, cleanliness and inner spiritual strength that are symbolised by the White Woman; from his crouching position among the cane she appears tall, distant, reaching to heaven like the religious bamboo-pole. She is strong-limbed and upright whilst he is weak, bent before the cane. Her eternal bamboo-stillness and steadiness contrasts with his eternal activity: she is removed from life whereas he is steeped in its flux and squalor. His silent call to her (as 'Shanti' – the word means 'peace') is the cry of the soul for release from life, a religious cry. But it is futile. The sunlight separates them, showing their differences, revealing her spiritual, social and physical superiority.

So he will chop her down to size, to possess her in another way, and in the dark, when the differences are not seen.

The fact that she comes to the canefield to watch the canecutters at their brutal work suggests that she is as fascinated by them as they are by her. She wants to be degraded secretly (the long lace frock is temptingly rich, and it hangs loose, suggestively; also the chaos of her hair), to be possessed and mutilated in the mud. The tragedy is as much hers for her desires too are prevented by social barriers. She can only stand and watch and fantasise, then go away. They pause and fantasise too before going back to the cane. Nothing is achieved.

The solitary canecutter sings, voicing the individual fantasy which is the collective fantasy. He is the priest whose words work on them, gathers to a pitch and sparks off a response which is the chorus of lust. The ritualistic song of the canecutters is a perverse replica of that of the Hindu ceremony – both of them, *inter alia,* are cries for fertility.

TRANSLATION:

White woman walks through the field to watch us at work/ Tall, straight, strong-limbed/ Hair sprinkled in wind like gold-dust/ Long lace frock loose on her body like bamboo-flag/ And her flesh, more than the hibiscus of early morning, soft and white and wet/ Flowering in her panties/ O Shanti! Shanti! Shanti!/ Wash this dirty skin in your dew/ Wipe it clean on your soft white petal!/ O Shanti! Shanti! Shanti!/ So my spirit calls, so it cries out for you/ When I peep out at you between cane-stems, strain my nose to catch your scent/ 'Bram-bram, bram-bram' – so my heart beats – I'm afraid you'll hear/ But daylight separates you and I, and this mud on my hands/ This sweat from my face, these rags on my back/ The entrance to your womb glows, a golden mesh of light, the sun seeds and sprouts there/ I'm too black to come there.

But when night comes, how I dream/ That your womb lies like a starapple burst open in the mud/ And of how I hold you down, shake up your waist/ Draw blood from your womb, daub it over your face/ Till you're dirty like me and you scream/ Like when cutlass slips and slices my leg, and you shake/ Like when snake twists round my foot, when we're cutting cane/ So I dream/ When night comes/ And mosquito wakes up from the bush/ Malabunta moves.

Boy have you ever dreamt her with her drawers down/ Boy have you ever worked her with your tongue/ Boy have you ever tasted her womb/ Soft and dripping like baigan-chokey!

SLAVE SONG

The slave addresses his Master (mentally of course). He asserts his manhood, his dignity and his instinct for survival through his surreptitious lust for the white woman, his Mistress. He will not be beaten down or reduced to utter impotence.

On one level his lust is obscene and revengeful: he can cuckold his Master by mentally degrading his Master's wife, dragging her down to his level of existence; that is, he can 'Africanize' her ('totempole her cunt', 'leave his teeth mark like a tattoo on her throat' – lines 32-3). He boasts that he can really act out the role of a cannibal (designated to him – line 15 – by his white superiors) by gaining life at her expense.

But such lust is also life-giving in a more poignant way, as the final verse makes out. His dream of her allows him to survive his condition of squalor – and she does not suffer since his conquest of her is merely mental. She is only a symbol through which to express his desire for life. On a deeper level the emotion trembles on the lyrical (e.g. lines 28-30: the imagined post-coital peace and his deliberate, sentimental evocation of a 'Noble Savage' Utopian ambience), though on the surface it seems disgustingly animal (the images of the crappau frog and camoudie snake). The images of gold within the poem ('goldmine', 'sunshine', 'honeypot', i.e. the pubic blondness of the white woman) play with this Utopian idea cynically ... and wistfully.

There is also an element of comic, mischievous laughter in the slave's celebration of his cock (cf. Medieval ithyphallics) which shows his remarkable strength of character and his intelligence – it makes him heroic almost – for it is humour in the face of utter suffering and cruelty. The gaiety, conveyed through imagery as well as rhythm, undermines the surface obscenity of his fantasy, and adds a further dimension to the psychology of the slave.

TRANSLATION:

Tie my hands up/ Pierce my eyes/ Haul my teeth out/ So I'll not bite./ Put chains around my neck/ Lash my feet tight/ Set your dogs to guard/ Morning till night –

But you can't stop my cock flooding in the goldmine/ Can't stop my cock splashing in the sunshine!

Whip me till I bleed/ Till I beg./ Tell me I'm an animal/ An African orang-utan/ Tell me I'm a cannibal/ Fit only for slaughter or hanging/ Slice one lip out/ One ear and one leg –

But you can't stop my cock dipping in the honeypot,/ Dripping at the tip and happy as a Hottentot!

Look how he leaps from bush to bush like a black toad/ Seeking out a waterhole/ Blind by the sunflare, tongue like a dust-bowl –/ See how he sips long and full and slow!

Till he's swollen and heavy, stubborn, dazed, full of sleep/ Like camoudie snake after swallowing a calf, stretched out in the grass, content/ Full of peace.../ Hibiscus bloom, a cool breeze blows/ And from a hill a waterflow/ Canaries singing soft and low...

It's so when you've done dreamt her pink nipples/ Totempoled her cunt/ Left your teeth mark like a tattoo in her throat!

She gives me thought/ She gives me wife/ So tear out my liver/ Or stake my heart/ I'll still have life.

LOVE SONG

Love Song moves from the wistful idyllic tone of the first stanza, in which the White Woman is conceived as night-cool, night-chaste and ethereal, to the deep self-disgust of the second stanza in which the canecutter recognises by contrast his own existence in scorching daylight filth – in other words, from the sensitivity to purity to the sensitivity to grime. The 'dut' ('dirt') he complains of in the second stanza is cane-ash: before cutting takes place the fields are set on fire to burn away the unwanted leaves of the caneplant. The canecutter is therefore steeped in ash as he chops away.

The third stanza sees the intensification of bitterness. Self-disgust gives way to a blasting anger and, at the same time, despair: the line 'work is never done, never done, never done' catches both moods. He becomes worked up, his emotion verges on hysteria and breakdown as he realizes the extremity of his suffering. This mental disintegration is correlated to what he sees as the physical and sexual disintegration resulting from his canecutting labour – 'tongue burnt', 'heart hurt', 'cutlass slips and cuts my cock'.

The fourth stanza sees a sudden shift in tone to one of immense relief and gratitude for the ending of the day, the ending of work and the coming of night. The rhythm changes from its previous incensed throbbing to a childish, joyous jingle.

The final stanzas are sentimental. The Guyanese peasant, when drunk to a degree that eliminates his capacity for violence, tends to become deeply reflective, melancholy, self-pitying, as tender and as helpless as a child. Here the intoxicated canecutter contemplates the coming of the White Woman in the night, a mother-figure who will suckle him and attend to his aching body. She is at the same time the splendidly sexual goddess who will repair the sexual damage involved in his daytime activity of canecutting. Of course she is only the stuff of dreams, but her image and his desire for her sustain him the next day when he awakens to the realities of plantation existence. On the other hand it also makes him frustrated, and his life is a constant flow of desire, and a constant realization of the unreality of his desire. He will remain dreaming in the mud and awakening to the mud, a tragic oscillation between fantasy and reality.

Line 2: The blue-saki is a Guyanese bird of mystical beauty, with sky-blue and sea-blue body and wings.

TRANSLATION:

Moon-eye/ Blue like blue-saki wing/ Moon-eye, all morning in my mind.

Black man covered with estate-ash/ His head hard and dry like calabash/ Dirt in his nostrils, in his ears/ Dirt in his soul, in his anus.

All/ day/ sun/ burns/ tongue/ burns/ all/ day/ throat/ cut/ heart/ hurt/ work's never done, never done, never done./ Hack! Hack! Hack! Hack!/ Cutlass slips and cuts your cock.

Thank God for six o'clock/ I go home/ And I'll bathe/ And I'll comb/ And I'll rock/ In hammock/ Cassava, pepperpot/ Drink some rum and coconut!

When my soul's soft and my eyes wet/ And the breeze blows and my eyes shut/ And the bottle has no more rum/ Then come/ And take me away, where/ there's no chain/ there's no cane/ Come with milk in your breast and your white throat bare/ With bangles on your hands and bells round your waist/ Come with oil and perfume and lace.

Moon-eye/ Blue like blue-saki wing/ Silk frock tumbles and splashes on my face like waterfall/ And you dance and you call/ In the night.

ELEGY

Elegy attempts to convey the tenderness, the lyrical potential, of Creole in imagery and rhythm. An old man wakes up on a cold morning to find that there's life around him (natural life – the calves struggling to suck, the blue-saki chirping) but not in himself. His youth is gone, and his woman, and his friends, and nothing makes sense. The atmosphere of death and breakdown of peasant order are conveyed in simple everyday peasant images: Jasmattie no longer beats clothes on the riverbank; her 'bellnay' (rolling-pin for making roti or chapati) and her 'puckni' (peasant instrument for getting the mud fireside started, like a bellows) are in disuse. And the bottomhouse is all cracked for there is no woman to plaster it over with fresh mud and manure. In the early morning the country kitchen is a bustle of activity and the absence of such activity is immediately strange to any peasant. The woman lights her fire, fetches water, fusses among her pots, rolls her dough, calls on the rest of the household to awaken, picks her way among the naked children who squat here and there in the kitchen, in the peculiar way that peasants squat, and who are barely awake, their heads supported dreamily in the palms of their hands. This early morning stupefaction, with a vague sense of the Mother's hectic movements and the smell of woodsmoke, fried fish and fresh dough is a distinguishing feature of any peasant's memory of childhood. In the poem the Old Man awakes and enters into such a childish stupefaction, and memories are unleashed.

As to the male friends of his youth, they're all gone – their cutlasses, their fishing nets, long laid down, and their sheep wandering loose. No-one tends the vegetable garden, a central peasant concern, and wild birds and animals feed and graze unhindered.

The poem can also be read as a lament for the incipient passing of the old rural order in Guyana with the coming of the new urbanized, westernized forms of life.

Lines 8-9: Guyanese country people are often known by their nicknames which reveal their physical or mental features and habits. 'Badman' – man notorious for violence or wickedness. 'Tiefman' –

robber, burglar, etc. 'Blackbattie' — someone with particularly black-tanned buttocks.

Line 15: 'Sapadilla' — a soft brown, deliciously juicy fruit. 'Bubby' — breasts.

Line 21: 'Bottomhouse' — the space underneath the house perched on stilts. The 'bottomhouse' is 'daubed' regularly with mud and manure to keep it smooth and uncracked — a woman's job.

TRANSLATION:

So you lean over the bannister, early cold morning/ Old man. Are you sick? What's the matter with you? What's wrong?/ And your hands are weak, trembling, and your mouth moves/ But there're no words, and your eye stares out at the field, long, long/ But you do not see the calves stir and struggle to suck/ And you do not hear the blue-saki's song high in the jamoon tree —/ It's old you're old, that's what it is.

Snakeneck, Fisheye, Badman, Richard/ Young yesterday all those boys, Thiefman, Blackarse, Goose/ Late late in the night you drank rum, you beat drums/ Roast crabs, curass, telling ghost stories till morning comes.../ And where are they? All laid up their nets, put down their cutlasses, all let their sheep loose/ All dead!/ And Jasmattie beating clothes on the river-bank — thump! thump! thump! thump!/ How her hands are strong, and her back straight and her breasts sweet sapidilla-brown!/ You remember how your throat lumped when you first saw her/ And how her young body leapt, leaked blood, when you rolled her on the ground? ...

All their slingshots are burst, all their fences broken/ Down, so animals graze unmolested in their vegetable gardens, and birds peck/ The fireside is cracked, and the bottomhouse, and no mouth blows the bellows, no hand works the rolling-pin/ And what makes things so?

60

NIGHTMARE

In *Nightmare,* the White Woman fantasises about being raped, degraded and mutilated by her Black servants who, according to her warped mentality, are no more than savage blood animals. The nocturnal atmosphere of Guyanese bush-life (stanza 4), one of horrible fertility and death, in some measure conditions her image of the Black.

In declaiming this piece, the canecutter shows his scorn of the White Woman's base image of him, and his tone of narration is full of irony and superior laughter ... his voice lingers melodramatically over the squalid details of her dream to show how extravagant and overdone they are.

The final line glances comically and perversely at the 'aubade' convention in which Medieval lovers lament the coming of the sun which disturbs their secret nocturnal joy. The White Woman awakens, wet with surreptitious sexual arousal and not with terror.

Line 6: 'Jigga': a severe itching and peeling of the flesh as a result of contact with putrid matter.

Line 10: 'Buss she tail' – a Guyanese expression (usually 'buss she tail wid licks', i.e. 'burst her tail with lashes') meaning to beat severely on the buttocks.

TRANSLATION:

Batter down the door!/ One gang of sweaty, stinking niggers/ Drag her off her bed/ Work upon her/ Crack her head/ Give her jigga/ Between her thighs.

They chase her backdam/ One gang of cane-stiff phalluses/ Lash her buttocks till they're black and blue/ Till she crawls through the mud and she bawls and she begs.

They haul her to the canal-bank like a bush-hog/ Cut her throat over the dark surging waters/ When they finish sucking they raise their red mouths to the moon/ And make song,

Deep in the night when crappau call and cush-cush/ Crawl down holes, lay their eggs in the earth/ When camoudie snake curls round calf that's just dropped [i.e. born]/ And black bats flap-flap-flap through the bush

Wet she awakes, cursing the daybreak!

MEN AND WOMEN

Men and Women deals with the pain of remorse. The peasant, like so many Guyanese peasants under the influence of rum, beat his wife, then later abandoned her with a hutch of children to support, a common fate for country women. Many years later, having wasted his money and life whoring, he returns, but she's old and feebleminded, a cripple almost, and she does not recognise him. And he's sorry as he remembers the brief happiness he gave her on their wedding night. But it's too late for him.

The poem seeks to represent the whole of Guyanese country life as one of aborted promises, hardships and cruelty – natural and human; the situation only redeemable by individual remorse and compassion.

Line 23: 'Dunlopilla bed' – a Dunlop (English-made, foam-mattressed) bed, the possession of which is rare, and a status symbol, in the countryside of Guyana where people sleep mostly on the floor. Here it symbolises the young couple's hope of marital comfort and wealth.

Line 3: Old country people all have amazingly cracked soles, because of course they're barefooted most of their lives, except on special occasions such as when they get married.

TRANSLATION:

So I'm sorry./ But when you've grown old, and your voice weak, and your mouth dribbling/ And the soles of your feet cracked/ It's too late/ To say sorry.

But I'm still sorry.

Because I drank rum and beat your/ Young, soft, wet-eyed face./ Because I made you pregnant year after year/ Nine mouths to feed, and I run off with my sweet woman/ Sport all my inheritance in a whore-house./ Because you had to work in the fields, from morning to nightfall/ Bruising up your small hand, and the sun peeling your skin./ Because when you sat down to roll pancakes, or to rock baby in hammock/ You didn't sing with gladness like other women/ How your mouth was sour like tamarind.

I've come back now, but now you're old/ And you don't know me/ How your mind's weak/ And your eyes dull/ But blood stirs in my body still when I look upon you/ Like a long time ago, when you were my midnight bride/ Bright, fresh, hopeful, and I lay you upon the Dunlop-pillow bed —/ Downstairs they were beating drums, they were singing love songs, they were dancing in the firelight! ...

And I'm truly sorry!

FOR MA

This poem, describing the bustle of a peasant household at daybreak, is a small tribute to the women of Guyana – the women who toil from daylight to midnight, cooking, cleaning, fetching water, rearing children, planting vegetables; the women who labour in the fields like mules; the women who endure poverty and the cruelties of men, and who yet, miraculously, manage to retain and transmit humour and vision and beauty.

The extraordinary richness of the Creole language defies adequate translation. A breathless, hectic line such as 'cutlass foh shaap wood foh chap fence foh build dat bull bruk dung' (line 11) becomes quite tame in standard English, the sinister assonance of 'cutlass', 'shaap', 'chap' and the battering alliteration of 'build bull bruk dung' (both devices re-enacting the meaning of the sentence) being lost in translation. Similarly the last line: there, the monosyllables trip over each other in their haste to complete the sentence, a sense of onward, tripping motion helped on by the internal assonance and rhymes ('en ... ay ... ow ... ap ... ch'; 'drap stap') as well as by the dance and tumble of Creole conjunctions and prefixes ('a ... an ... a ... na'). This Creole choreography becomes lame in translation.

TRANSLATION:

Roll roti! roll roti! roll roti! roll roti!/ Curry cooking in the karahie/ Bora boiling with the bagee/ Woodsmoke sweet in my nose like incense/ Wake up, wake up the lot of you, wake up you children, wake up you man/ With the sunshine in your eyes and the river flowing/ And brown doves bursting from the trees, and the kiskadees/ And the whole savannah swimming green and glowing!

Water to fetch, bottom-house to daub afresh, bucket to mend, clothes to beat/ Wake up you children, work's not done, work's to do/ Cutlass to sharpen, wood to chop, fence to rebuild that the bull broke down,/

What's that man stretching his hand and yawning for!/ Hear how the cows bawl in the yard, they're swollen with milk/ The goats groan, they want to graze, and sheep keep coughing./ Wake up you lot, wake up, there's no time to cry, there's no time to laugh/ Hens are laying, cows are bearing, there's no time to stop!

SLAVEWOMAN'S SONG

TRANSLATION:

You howl/ Hear how you howl/ Tell me why you howl/ Tell me, no?/ Is it child?/ Did they take away your child?/ What have they done with your child/ That you knock your head with stone/ Bite your hand like dogbone?

Or is it your husband you're crying for girl?/ What have they done to him/ That you daub your face with cow dung/ Pierce your eyes and chop your tongue?/ Have they thrown him into the Demerara river, fed him to the alligators?

Is it your mother? Your father? Africa?/ Or are you pregnant by Massa?

You howl/ Hear how you howl/ Tell me why you howl/ Tell me, no?

BROWN SKIN GIRL

The white man, in the days of colonial rule, took Guyanese women for his mistress or his whore, at his leisure. Now, after two centuries of domination, some Guyanese women 'willingly' give themselves to the white man in a new kind of prostitution. They do so out of a deep feeling of inferiority. Ashamed of their history and their habits, they seek out the culture of the white man, one perceived to be superior in manners and material. For the women, this quest for 'civilisation' can only be realised through giving their bodies: what else have they to offer the white man? What else is he capable of taking from them?

Of course such 'prostitution' is a blow to the ego of the Guyanese male, since it is a judgement on his capacity to satisfy, sexually and materially. *Brown Skin Girl* is an expression of his pathetic, sentimental response to being abandoned. And yet he is not entirely blameless. There is a Guyanese folk song which celebrates the sexual uncouthness of the Guyanese male towards the female:

> Brown skin girl
> Go home and mind baby.
> Brown skin girl
> Go home and mind baby.
> I'm going away
> On a sailing boat
> And if I don't come back
> Throw away the damn baby.

('Throw away' meaning abortion.) My *Brown Skin Girl* depicts the Guyanese male at the receiving end of such cruel desertion and sexual disdain. It revises the folk song in the light of present-day emigration to America and the Americanisation of Guyana.

Line 7: 'Mar' – the starch from boiled rice, fed to dogs and to poor people.

Line 12: 'Kreketeh' – disease-bearing gutter-snails.

TRANSLATION:

Go, go to America, brown skin girl/ Meet white man./ You will learn/
To speak properly, dress, drive car/ Hold knife and fork in your hand:/
The mud, the canal, the canefield gone/ And I with ricebowl drinking
mar/ I with ricebowl thinking far.

Go, go to America, brown skin girl/ Make money, make children/ Move
smooth, stand tall:/ Cockroach, kreketeh/ Mosquito, there's none
there/ To break your life, to make you crawl/ Nor I with fishnet waiting
tide/ Dreams like bleeding deep inside.

TWO CULTURES

The situation is a common one in Guyana: a humorous confrontation between the old peasant type and the new urbanized and travelled young Guyanese who has recently returned from England, perhaps on a holiday, or more likely under deportation orders. The young man affects white manners and white speech in a show of superiority, and also to catch the eye of the young country girls, who, like country girls all over the world, are attracted by the country boy who has returned from foreign parts all polished and chic.

The old man sees through the fraud. As far as he's concerned no Guyanese can ever evolve into 'whiteness'. The boy's father is a peasant farmer like the rest of them, and the boy can never develop away from his roots. His 'guts' (what he eats, what he is) are as Guyanese as ever: his teeth are as yellow as dhall (the staple diet of Indo-Guyanese) and his tongue black like cassareep (the ingredient of a staple Afro-Guyanese food, pepperpot).

The old man's attitude is healthy in so far as it debunks the more trivial 'white' aspirations of the young Guyanese (flashy speech, flashy clothes, etc.) and it reminds him of his roots in something more serious and substantial: the physical, manual contact with the earth which the boy's own father is involved in. But at the same time the old man's attitude is strangely colonialist and reactionary. He believes that Guyanese are Guyanese, and the English are the English: one race is inferior to the other, parity between them being unthinkable. The old man believes that the White Woman would never stop so low as to mate with the black boy (i.e., the meeting and interaction of the two cultures on the deepest and most equal level, the sexual level). And he adopts the current white myth (and previous colonialist myth) of blacks being mere muggers and petty criminals. Despite a decade of liberation (Guyana was made independent in 1966) the old Guyanese type (especially the Indo-Guyanese) remains as servile as ever, understandably, after centuries of domination.

Line 2: Every lunchtime, those Guyanese with transistors tune in to the BBC World Service for its news broadcast. It is a sacred ritual, an acknowledgement of the superiority of the White Man in matters of seriousness and truth.

Line 23: The Indo-Guyanese is fiercely protective towards his female children. This paternal instinct defines him.

TRANSLATION:

'Just listen to the boy talking/ Like BBC!/ Look how he walks/ Like white man/ Cork-hat on his head, wrist-watch on his hand!/ Isn't your father called Dabydeen who plants vegetables near Blackbush Pass?/ Doesn't he cut with a sickle and dig with a fork?/ Doesn't he sell in the marketplace, plantain and corn?/ Well fuck me/ Whose child are you then?/ Well I've never seen anything like this since I was born!

He went to England for a couple of days, illegally/ And he eyed up one or two white women/ But what would those sweet waterlily seeds/ Want to have with a hungry-bellied Blackbush weed/ Like you, how your teeth are yellow like lentils/ And your tongue black like molasses!/ They should have spat, vomited upon you, beat you with whips!/ It's trash like you who spoil those good white people's country/ Mugging and breaking and entering and stealing their property!

So you think you can come back here and play big shot/ Impress us with your cigarettes, apples and all that?/ We may be poor country people but we've got our pride:/ Just you touch my girl-child, and I'll split your arse!

ILLUSTRATIONS:

'Britannia and the Natives.' By R. Smirke. In James Montgomery, *The Abolition of the Slave Trade, A Poem* (London, 1814), opp. page 19.

A piece of sugar cane. In *The Sugar Cane,* Vol. V, 1873.

'The Execution and Breaking on the Rack.' Anonymous engraving, 1793. In J. Stedman, *Narrative of a Five Years's Expedition against the Revolted Negroes of Surinam, in Guiana* (2 vols, 1796), Vol. II, opp. page 296.

'A Rebel Negro.' Engraved by Bartolozzi, 1794. In Stedman, *Narrative of a Five Years' Expedition against the Revolted Negroes of Surinam, in Guiana,* Vol. II, opp. page 88.

'A Female Negro Slave with a Weight Chained to her Ankle.' Engraved by Francis Bartolozzi, 1795. In Stedman, *Narrative of a Five Years' Expedition against the Revolted Negroes of Surinam, in Guiana,* Vol. I, opp. page 15.

'A Surinam Planter in his Morning Dress.' Engraved by William Blake, 1793. In Stedman, *Narrative of a Five Years' Expedition against the Revolted Negroes of Surinam, in Guiana,* Vol. II, opp. page 6.

SLAVE SONG – POSTSCRIPT

Twenty-one years on, I encounter the poems, shocked by the nakedness and obscenity of expression. I was reading *Sir Gawain/The Pearl* etc. whilst writing some of *Slave Song* and was taken by the muscularity of the northern alliterative language. *Slave Song* was a dark anti-Romance. Today, I distance myself from what Wilson Harris called 'the pornography of Empire.' 'This thing of darkness I don't acknowledge mine.'

What I'm happier to take credit for is the apparatus of the Introduction, notes and translations, which appear to be peculiar midwives to the poems, seeking to strangle them at birth. The influence of the eighteenth century is apparent, whether didactic poetry like Grainger's *Sugar Cane* with its masses of notes and explanations, or editions of the Classics in which thirty pages of Ovid or Horace are accompanied by three hundred pages of notes by editors showing off their erudition, holding up farthing candles to sunlight (Pope's *Dunciad* parodies the practice). T.S. Eliot's 'spoof' notes were also in mind, *Slave Song* being so much creole wasteland without indigenous literary antecedents or literary tradition to allude to and quote from – hence the resort to the Classical and Medieval writers, to T.S. Eliot etc. The citations, however, were not meant to be hostile, but acts of homage to great writers. We may have come to the Classics through demeaning ways, the plantocracy naming their slaves Horace or Virgil or Caesar, but why now deny ourselves the merriment of Catullus or the grief of Sophocles? And Grainger, for all his validation of slavery, was the first major British poet to describe the enormous natural forces of the Caribbean landscape.

Finally, the apparatus of notes and translations was an attempt to be poet, editor and translator, to resist the commerce of consuming 'third-world' produce. But I was young and idealistic and silly then. After twenty-one years of meagre royalties, I'm ripe for exploitation, so please buy this book.

DD

ABOUT THE AUTHOR

David Dabydeen was born in Guyana. He read English at Cambridge, taught at the University of Warwick, and is presently Guyana's Ambassador to China. His poetry has won the Commonwealth Poetry Prize. His fiction has been shortlisted for the John Llewelyn Rhys Prize, the James Tait Black Memorial Prize and the International Impac Dublin Award, and received the Guyana Prize, the Raja Rao Prize and the Sabga Caribbean Award.

ALSO AVAILABLE FROM PEEPAL TREE

Turner
ISBN: 978190071568 3, pp. 84, pub. 1994, 2002; £7.99

David Dabydeen's "Turner" is a long narrative poem written in response to JMW Turner's celebrated painting "Slavers Throwing Overboard the Dead & Dying". Dabydeen's poem focuses on what is hidden in Turner's painting, the submerged head of the drowning African. In inventing a biography and the drowned man's unspoken desires, including the resisted temptation to fabricate an idyllic past, the poem brings into confrontation the wish for renewal and the inescapable stains of history, including the meaning of Turner's painting.

"A major poem, full of lyricism and compassion, which gracefully shoulders the burden of history and introduces us to voices from the past whose voices we have all inherited" – Caryl Phillips

The Intended
ISBN: 9781845230135; pp. 246; pub. 1991, 2005; £8.99

The narrator of *The Intended* is twelve when he leaves his village in rural Guyana to come to England. There he is abandoned into social care, but seizes every opportunity to follow his aunt's farewell advice: "...but you must tek education...pass plenty exam." With a scholarship to Oxford, and an upper-class white fiancée, he has unquestionably arrived, but at the cost of ignoring the other part of his aunt's farewell: "you is we, remember you is we." First published almost fifteen years ago, *The Intended*'s portrayal of the instability of identity and relations between whites, African-Caribbeans and Asians in South London is as contemporary and pertinent as ever. As an Indian from Guyana, the narrator is seen as a "Paki" by the English, and as some mongrel hybrid by "real" Asians from India and Pakistan; as sharing a common British "Blackness" whilst acutely conscious of the real cultural divisions between Africans and Indians back in Guyana. At one level a moving semi-autobiographical novel, *The Intended* is also a sophisticated postcolonial text with echoes of *Heart of Darkness*.

Disappearance
ISBN: 9781845230142; pp.180; pub. 1993, 2005; £8.99

A young Afro-Guyanese engineer comes to a coastal Kentish village as part of a project to shore up its crumbling sea-defences. He boards with an old English woman, Mrs Rutherford, and through his relationship with her discovers that beneath the apparent placidity and essential Englishness of this village, violence and raw emotions are not far below the surface, along with echoes of the imperial past. In the process, he is forced to reconsider his perceptions of himself and his native Guyana, and to question his engineer's certainties in the primacy of the rational. This richly intertextual novel makes reference to the work of Conrad, Wilson Harris and VS Naipaul to set up a multi-layered dialogue concerning the nature of Englishness, the legacy of Empire and different perspectives on the nature of history and reality.

"An electrifying array of surmises about how the imperial past has affected everyone in Britain today" – *Scotsman*

The Counting House
ISBN: 9781845230159; pp. 180; pub. 1996, 2005; £8.99

Set in the early nineteenth century, *The Counting House* follows the lives of Rohini and Vidia, a young married couple struggling for survival in a small, caste-ridden Indian village who are seduced by the recruiter's talk of easy work and plentiful land if they sign up as indentured labourers to go to British Guiana. There, however, they discover a harsh fate as "bound coolies" in a country barely emerging from the savage brutalities of slavery. Having abandoned their families and a country that seems increasingly like a paradise, they must come to terms with their problematic encounters with an Afro-Guyanese population hostile to immigrant labour, with rebels such as Kampta who has made an early abandonment of Indian village culture, and confront the truths of their uprooted condition.

"Beautifully written... Dabydeen's grace, as a poet turned novelist, is to give his characters' imaginations and inner lives voices in prose... This is a marvelous novel" — Michele Roberts, *Independent on Sunday*

Our Lady of Demerara
ISBN: 9781845230692; pp. 288; pub. 2004, 2008; £9.99

At 30, drama critic Lance Yardley is already a seedy wreck of a man, spending his nights in the back streets of Coventry looking for prostitutes. A working-class boy brought up in a broken home on a council estate, he has sought escape in literature and through his marriage to an actress, the great-granddaughter of a 19th-century Englishman who made his fortune from the sugar plantations in Guyana. At first Elizabeth attracts Yardley, but their differences of class exacerbate the mutual hatred that grows between them. Later he is drawn to a mysterious Indian girl, Rohini. She seems shy, but sells her body to customers when her boss goes out of town. When she dies suddenly, the victim of a strange ritualistic murder, Yardley decides to decamp abroad for a while. He goes to Guyana, not least because he wants to learn more about an Irish priest who as an old man has been a priest in Coventry, but as a young man had worked as a missionary in Guyana. The priest's fragmented journals seem to offer Yardley some possible answers to his own spiritual malaise, but the Guyana he discovers provokes more questions than answers.

"a brooding, powerful novel of unusual ambition."

The Telegraph

Ed. Kevin Grant
The Art of David Dabydeen
ISBN: 9781900715102; pp. 231; pub. 1997; £12.99

In this volume, leading scholars discuss Dabydeen's poetry and fiction in the context of the politics and culture of Britain and the Caribbean. The essays explore his concern with the plurality of Caribbean experience; the dislocation of slavery and indenture; migration and the consequent divisions in the Caribbean psyche. In particular, the focus is on Dabydeen's aesthetic practice as a consciously post-colonial writer; his exploration of the contrasts between rural creole and standard English; the power of language to subvert accepted realities; his use of multiple masks as ways of dealing with issues of identity; and the play of destabilizing techniques within his narrative strategies.

"Part of the usefulness is that the essays overlap, build on, and disagree with one another. They bring out Dabydeen's recurring themes, autobiographical material, and the links among his scholarly publications, interviews, and creative writings." – Bruce King, *World Literature Today*

Eds Lynne Macedo and Kampta Karran
No Land, No Mother: Essays on the Work of David Dabydeen
ISBN: 9781845230203, pp. 236; pub. 2007; £12.99

The essays in this collection focus on the rich dialogue carried out in David Dabydeen's critically acclaimed body of writing. Dialogue across diversity and the simultaneous habitation of multiple arenas are seen as dominant characterics of his work. Essays by Aleid Fokkema, Tobias Döring, Heike Härting and Madina Tlostanova provide rewardingly complex readings of Dabydeen's *Turner*, locating it within a revived tradition of Caribbean epic. Lee Jenkins and Pumla Gqola explore Dabydeen's fondness for intertextual reference, his dialogue with canonic authority and ideas about the masculine. Michael Mitchell, Mark Stein, Christine Pagnoulle and Gail Low focus on his more recent fiction. Looking more closely at Dabydeen's Indo-Guyanese background, this collection complements the earlier *The Art of David Dabydeen*.